Bean

Barrie Watts

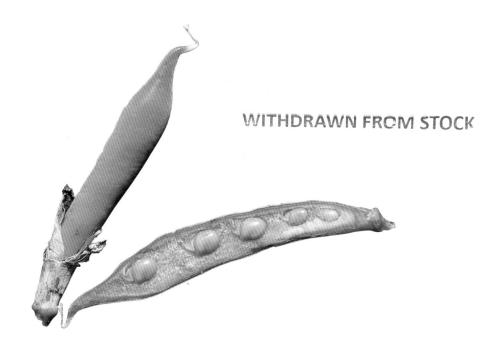

W
FRANKLIN WATTS
LONDON•SYDNEY

This edition 2007
First published in 2004 by Franklin Watts
338 Euston Road, London NW1 3BH

Franklin Watts Australia
Level 17/207 Kent Street, Sydney, NSW 2000

© Barrie Watts 2004

Editor: Kate Newport
Art director: Jonathan Hair
Photographer: Barrie Watts
Illustrator: David Burroughs

A CIP catalogue record for this book
is available from the British Library

ISBN 978 0 7496 7360 4

Dewey classification: 583.74

Printed in China

Franklin Watts is a division of Hachette Children's Books.

How to use this book

Watch It Grow has been specially designed to cater for a
range of reading and learning abilities. Initially children may
just follow the pictures. Ask them to describe in their own
words what they see. Other children will enjoy reading the
single sentence in large type, in conjunction with the pictures.
This single sentence is then expanded in the main text. More
adept readers will be able to follow the text and pictures by
themselves through to the conclusion of the life cycle.

Contents

Beans grow from seeds.

This bean seed is about 15 mm long. A new bean plant will grow from it. It has a hard, tough skin that protects the inside parts of the seed from drying out.

Inside the seed is a food store.
Bean seeds are kept in a cool, dry
place during the winter until they
are ready to be planted.

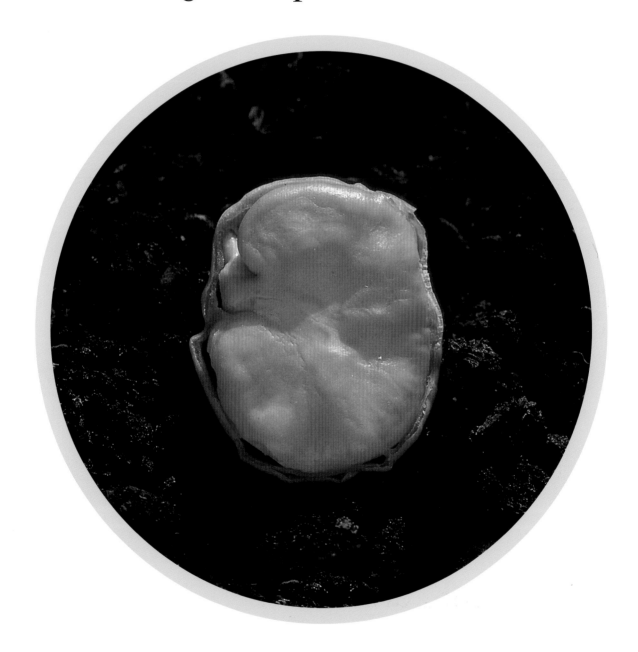

The bean is planted.

The seed is planted when the weather becomes warmer in the spring. The seed needs warmth and water to grow into a plant.

As soon as the seed is planted, the moist soil starts to soften the skin. Water reaches the inside of the seed and it starts to swell. The seed skin splits.

The bean sprouts.

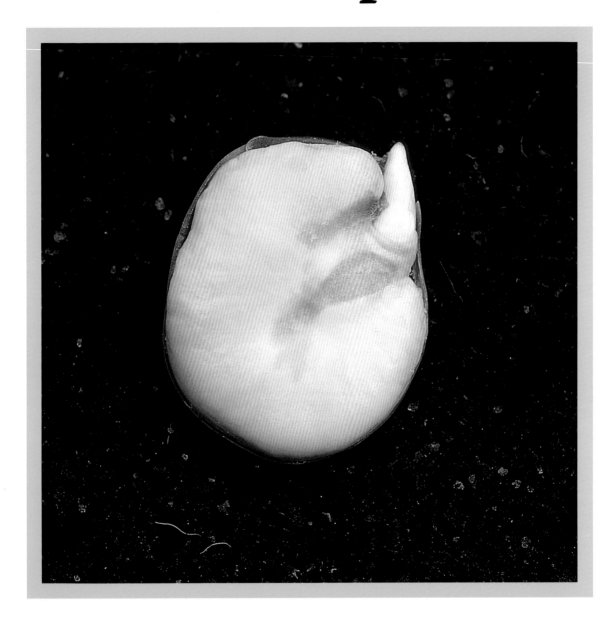

As the skin softens and splits,
the seed is able to grow a tiny
root from its top.

At first the root grows upwards, but soon it turns round and grows down into the soil. It begins to take in **moisture** and **nutrients** from the soil.

The seed leaves start to grow.

After a week, a pair of leaves, called **seed leaves,** emerge from the seed and grow towards the surface of the soil.

The seed leaves are folded down so they do not get damaged as they push through the soil. **Moisture** collected by the new roots helps the leaves grow.

The seed leaves push upwards.

The **seed leaves** grow on a stalk which pushes them through the soil. When they reach the surface, the leaves begin to open out.

As it grows, the plant uses the supply of food in the seed. When it is fully grown it will make its own food.

The proper leaves grow.

The **seed leaves** absorb sunlight. The sunlight combines with water from the roots to make food for the plant. This is called **photosynthesis**.

With this extra food the plant can
grow a stalk and its proper leaves.
The proper leaves have thin tubes
called **veins** in them. Food is passed
around the plant along the veins.

The root grows.

By now, the bean plant has grown many more roots under the soil. Tiny hairs on the roots take in more **moisture** and **nutrients** from the soil. The more nutrients the seed gets, the quicker it will grow. The network of roots also anchors the plant into the ground, enabling it to grow tall and strong.

The stalk is strong.

The bean plant's stalk grows upwards and is thin and strong. It is hollow and is made from tough **flexible** fibres. It has to be strong enough to carry all the plant's leaves, flowers and seeds without breaking.

Just below the stalk's green skin are **veins.** The veins carry water and food between the leaves and the root.

The flowers grow.

About two weeks after being planted, the plant begins to grow flower buds. They grow at the top of the plant.

As the stalk gets taller the plant continues to grow flower buds. The first flowers open up about 10 days after they first appear as buds.

Bees visit the flowers.

When the flowers open, they make **nectar** and **pollen.** The flowers put out a strong scent to attract bees and insects. Bees then visit the flowers in search of food.

To get to the nectar, bees have to brush past the **stamen** that carries the pollen. They then carry the pollen to the **stigma** of another flower and pollinate it.

The flower dies.

After pollination the flower dies.
The petals start to wither and fall
off. The plant is now five weeks old
and begins to grow seedpods.

There are usually between six and 10 seedpods on a bean plant. The flowers that are not pollinated will die without growing into a seedpod.

The seedpod grows.

The seedpod gets bigger. Inside
the pod are the seeds. They grow
by taking food from the plant,
using the **veins** in the stalk.

The young seeds are easily damaged by insects, and need to be protected. The inside of the pod is soft and hairy. The outer skin is tough to stop the seeds from drying out.

The plant dies.

About 12 weeks after being planted, the seedpods reach their full size, about 200 mm long. The plant then dies. Many seedpods are harvested for people to eat the seeds.

Other seeds are kept and planted the following spring to grow new bean plants. If the pods are left, they split and the seeds fall to the ground to grow into new plants.

Word bank

Flexible - When something is easy to bend, like a piece of wire, it is called flexible.

Moisture - When something is wet, like soil, it has a lot of moisture in it.

Nectar - A sweet, sugary liquid that attracts bees and other insects to flowers. Bees make honey from nectar.

Nutrients - Substances in the soil that help plants to grow.

Photosynthesis - When leaves make food for the plant by absorbing sunlight and taking in water from their roots, it is called photosynthesis.

Pollen - A fine yellow powder made by the male parts of a flower.

Seed leaves - The first leaves that grow on a plant. When proper leaves begin to grow, seed leaves turn yellow and die.

Stamen - The part of the flower that produces pollen.

Stigma - The female part of a flower that receives pollen. When this happens, the flower is pollinated and seedpods and seeds start to grow.

Veins - The tiny tubes in a leaf or in the stalk that carry food and water around the plant.

Life cycle

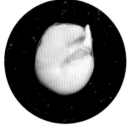

Soon after planting, the seed skin splits, and grows a root.

After 12 weeks the seedpods reach their full size and the plant dies.

After a week, a pair of seed leaves emerge and grow towards the surface of the soil.

The seedpod gets bigger. Inside the pod are the seeds.

The seed leaves grow on a stalk which pushes them through the soil.

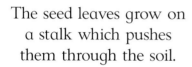

After pollination the flower dies. Five weeks after planting, the plant grows seedpods.

Two weeks after planting, the plant begins to grow flower buds. The flowers make nectar.

The nectar attracts insects that carry the pollen to other flowers and pollinate them.

Index